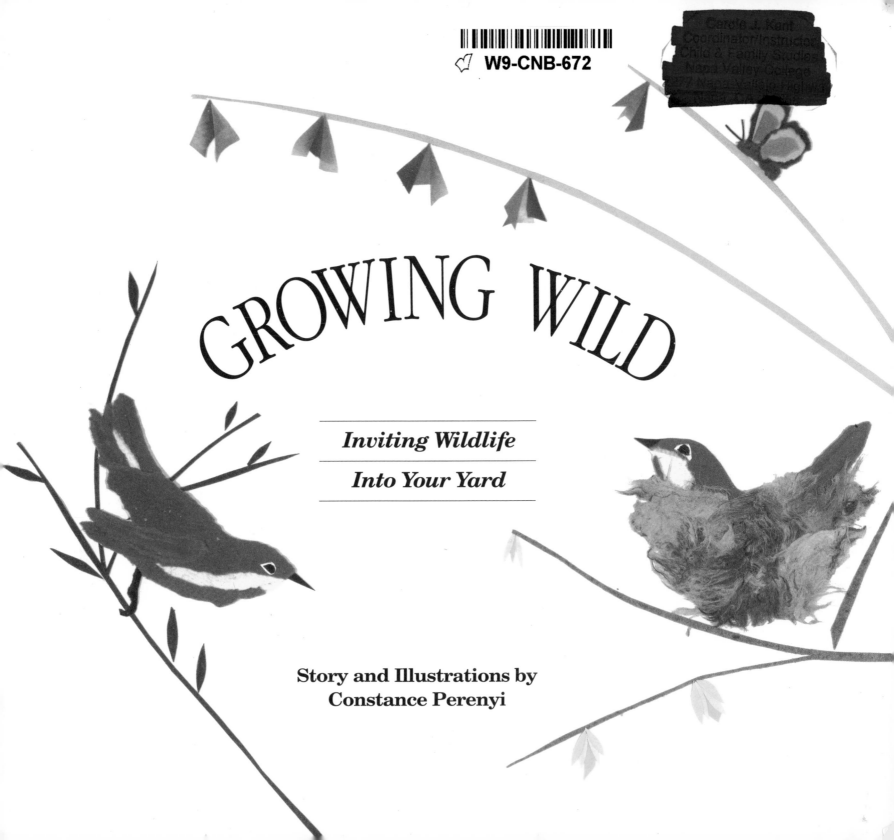

W9-CNB-672

Carole J. Kent
Coordinator/Instructor
Child & Family Studies
Napa Valley College

GROWING WILD

Inviting Wildlife

Into Your Yard

**Story and Illustrations by
Constance Perenyi**

This book is for my grandmother,

Katherine Morrell Perenyi

Published by
Beyond Words Publishing, Inc.

13950 NW Pumpkin Ridge Rd.
Hillsboro, OR 97123 USA
Phone (503) 647-5109
Toll Free 1-800-284-WORD

Printed in Mexico by: Impresora Donneco, S.A. de C.V.
Design: Principia Graphica
Typesetting: The TypeSmith

This book is printed on recycled paper.
ISBN: 0-941831-60-4 (hard cover)
ISBN: 0-941831-63-9 (soft cover)
Library of Congress card number: 91-070341

Copyright © 1991 by Constance Perenyi

All rights reserved. No part of this book may
be reproduced or transmitted in any form or by
any means, electronic or mechanical, including photo-
copying, recording, or by any information storage and
retrieval system, without the written permission of the
publisher, except where permitted by law.

The images in *Growing Wild* are collages of cut
and torn paper, crafted by the author. The author
is available for school presentations for *Growing Wild* and
can be contacted through the publisher.

Once upon a time

    (not really long ago, really)

In a land far away

    (not so far, actually —

    maybe your neighborhood

    or mine)

There was a perfect lawn . . .

Not just one perfect lawn,

but many.

Together, these squares of bright green

grass marched across the neighborhood.

All the lawns were proud to be perfect.

But they were also very,

very lonely.

They could remember a time
before the fences and the streets
when there was a different kind of green.
Trees and wildflowers and long free grasses
waved with the wind to greet
animals high and low.

Then everything changed. People began to saw down

trees and build tall fences. When the wild grasses

were cut, most of the animals left to find other homes.

But sometimes, even then, a robin visited

to look for worms.

She was a welcome sight,

a bright spot of color

on

the

perfectly

green

grass.

She never stayed long, though.

Without trees,

   she had nowhere

   to build a nest;

and without berries or insects,

   she had nothing to feed her young.

And when she left,

   the perfect lawns seemed lonelier than ever.

One day, just
a few years ago,
a small house
in the middle of a
large perfect lawn
was put up for sale.

For Sale!

The people in the house moved
and took their lawn mower,
grass trimmers, and all the sprays
they used to kill bugs and weeds.

At first there was nothing but an empty

house and a big empty yard.

But an amazing thing happened:

the big empty lawn

didn't stay empty for long.

At first, the grass started to

grow.

It got taller

and taller

and soon went to seed.

In a short time
other plants grew too.

The neighbors called them weeds,
but we all know a weed
is just a plant people don't
want in their perfect lawns.

11

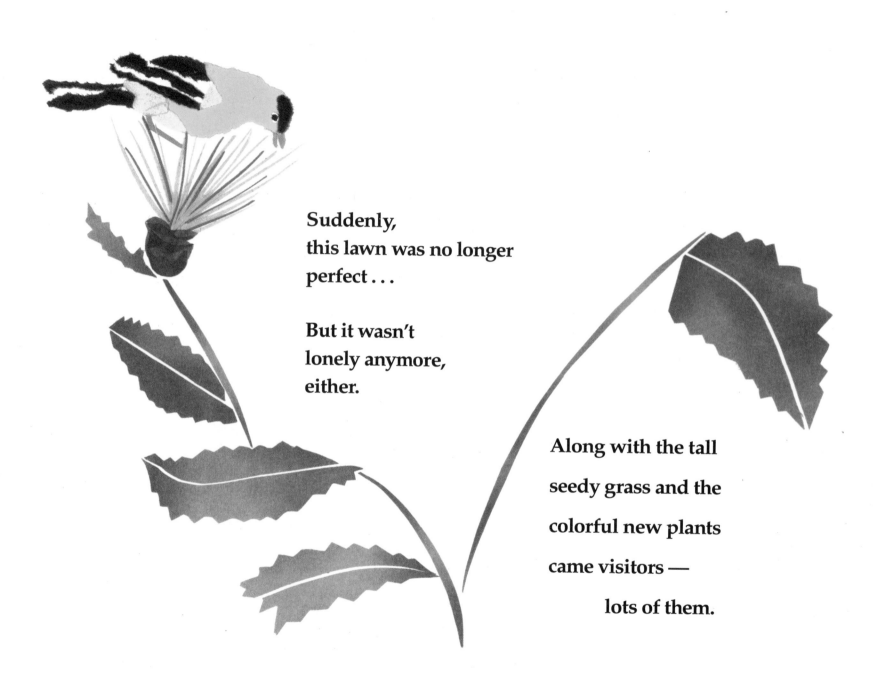

Suddenly,
this lawn was no longer
perfect . . .

But it wasn't
lonely anymore,
either.

Along with the tall

seedy grass and the

colorful new plants

came visitors —

lots of them.

12

Birds flew from far and wide to
feast on seeds. Bright flowers welcomed
honeybees, and butterflies flitted across the yard.
Perfect lawns
all around looked on
in wonder.

By the end of summer,

the wild yard with its empty house was sold.

"At last," said the neighbors. "Now someone will mow that awful lawn."

But what would happen to the yard?
Was it destined to be
perfect and lonely
again?

No, the yard was in luck.

The people who moved
into the little house
loved the creatures who
kept the tall grass company.

The people also knew they
could make the yard even better.
It would be a perfect garden
for all their new friends.

First they planted trees.

Some would keep their leaves all year;

others would be bare in the winter.

But they would

provide food and shelter

for garden animals.

Next, down came the fence

and up went a long hedge.

Bushy branches full
of berries — color in winter
and plenty of treats for the birds.

Parts of the garden
grow wild.

Other areas are
mowed close.

Now the robin has
a place to stay
as long as she wants.

20

The garden has become a home for
animals throughout the year.

During the summer,

flowers attract hummingbirds.

The birdbath is always full,
and the garden splashes with
cheerful activity.

Crisp days and dewy
spider webs are
sure signs
of fall.

Birds as bright as autumn leaves arrive in the garden. Some stop for a short visit as they fly south. Others stay as the days shorten and the air chills.

In the years past, winter was an especially lonely time in the yard. Nothing seemed alive. Everything looked flat and cold.

But now, the garden bustles with birds in the feeders and squirrels on the snow. Even the frost seems to sparkle with life.

Ever so slowly, the sun grows stronger.
Birds build nests and sing to
announce the coming of
spring.

Buds and flowers and fresh green leaves bring color to the new season. These are warm and happy days in the garden.

And what, you might wonder,

has become of all the other

perfect lawns in the neighborhood?

Well, nature has a wonderful

way of taking care of friends:

birds spread seed,

squirrels bury nuts.

Soon, flowers sprout and trees take root everywhere. There is no longer a perfect lawn in sight, and the neighbors don't know what to do. They have come to like the new people on the block and even to admire their colorful garden.

In the end, the yards make
the decision. Tired of being perfect,
they don't want to be
lonely anymore.

So the neighborhood grows wild, too.

No longer a block of perfectly square

lawns, it has become one big

garden, a perfect place

to live happily ever after.

Catalogue of specific plants and **animals** listed by page

Contact your local Cooperative Extension agency to learn more about plants adapted to your area.

HOW TO GARDEN FOR WILDLIFE:

An introductory guide for adults and children gardening together.

Why do we garden for wildlife? As human populations expand, there is less land and fewer natural resources for wildlife. Some wild animals adjust well to being close to humans. Others do not, and their dwindling numbers have been forced into retreat.

When we invite wildlife into our yards, we help to reverse this trend in a small but significant way. Most modern gardening practices, especially ones devoted to maintaining perfect lawns, exclude wildlife. But by changing the way we garden, we can create a place for wild animals that might not otherwise survive in our cities, suburbs, or even rural areas. Best of all, people of all ages benefit from this kind of sanctuary as much as plants and animals do.

The main goal of gardening for wildlife is to create habitat, which means providing sources of food, shelter and water for wild animals. Here is an introduction to creating an animal-friendly garden. For more information, refer to the resources listed on the last page.

GETTING STARTED
• First, learn about the plants and animals in your area. Do you already have wild visitors in your yard? If so, can you identify them? Field guides are excellent resources to help you recognize what you see.

• Learn what creatures you might expect as you invite more animals into your yard. For example, if you live in the far western regions of North America, you probably will not attract a bird like the northern cardinal no matter how hard you try. Again, field guides can help you learn about an animal's natural range.

• Discover the plants and animals that are native to your area. Many of these have had an especially hard time surviving in our changing environment. Whenever possible, plant native species of trees, shrubs and wildflowers. And try to learn what it is that native animals need to survive. With careful planning, you might be able to provide for these species in your wildlife garden.

DESIGNING A GARDEN
• You don't need to have a large space to garden for wildlife. What you do need is variety. By offering many different plants in your yard, you increase your chances of attracting wild animals.

• Start tall with trees and work down in height to shrubs, grasses, ground covers and lawn. In nature, wild areas feature this kind of diversity. Different levels support different animals, and in this way your garden becomes a multi-storied dwelling for wildlife.

• Despite their popularity in American cities and suburbs, perfectly groomed lawns do not provide habitat for many animals. Furthermore, they require hours of maintenance and gallons of valuable water. However, you do not have to let your entire lawn grow wild to attract animals. Areas of lawn can be integrated into your overall garden design as long as you create natural areas for wildlife as well.

THE IMPORTANCE OF ORGANIC GARDENING

• In gardening for wildlife, it is critical to avoid using pesticides. These poisons affect all animals indiscriminately and contaminate the ground water. Furthermore, chemical applications can be costly, especially if you enroll in a spray program that requires regular and often unnecessary applications. You end up paying a lot, the environment pays even more, but the pesticide manufacturers and spray companies make out like bandits.

• The variety of plants in a natural garden helps defeat the pests which can infest "monocultures" — areas that feature only one kind of plant. The wildlife in your yard can help, too. Birds devour insects, especially in the spring and summer when they need extra protein to feed their young. Garter snakes eat slugs, and a single bat can consume more than 3,000 mosquitos in one night.

HOW TO PROVIDE SHELTER
IN YOUR GARDEN HABITAT

• Wild animals need shelter to rest, to escape predators, and to raise their young. You can help by providing a variety of plants. Include both deciduous and evergreen species in your garden, especially those native to your area.

• Whenever possible, let plants grow in their natural form. Dense, irregular branches provide much better cover for wildlife than do neatly trimmed trees and shrubs.

• Leave old or dead trees in your yard if they do not pose a safety hazard. These offer valuable shelter to birds like flickers, woodpeckers and chickadees that nest in the cavities of old or dead wood. Insects often live under the bark and are an important food source for other wildlife.

• Many animals including birds, amphibians, and insects need to find their shelter on the ground. If you can choose a site in your garden to build piles of stones or brush, ground-dwelling animals are sure to take advantage of them.

• To encourage birds to nest in your yard, hang nesting boxes in trees or on your house. Choose sites that do not receive too much direct sun in the heat of the day. And be sure to build or select models that are easily cleaned and have appropriately sized openings. The smaller the hole the better for birds like wrens and chickadees. There is also less chance of the intended occupants being evicted by aggressive starlings or English house sparrows.

• If you live near a body of fresh water, you might be able to invite bats into your yard by hanging a specially-designed bat house. For more information, write to Bat Conservation International, P.O. Box 16203, Austin, TX 78716.

PROVIDING FOOD SOURCES

• Again, diversity is key. When you choose a variety of plants, you ensure a food supply throughout the year and encourage self-sufficiency in wildlife.

• Berried plants help many animals survive the winter. Crab apples, hawthorns and mountain ash are good choices for trees. Birds thrive on the fruits of pyracantha, Virginia creeper and American bittersweet. They will even eat brightly colored rose hips.

• If you want to keep some of the fruit in your yard off-limits to birds, cover plants with netting and be sure to harvest the fruit as soon as possible.

• Seeds and nuts nourish wildlife. You can start high with deciduous trees such as alder, birch and oak and conifers like pine and fir. Let plants at lower levels go to seed. Common garden flowers like cosmos and sunflower attract many birds, but nothing is as appealing to them as weeds. If you feel generous, let some of your yard grown really wild. The seeds of crabgrass, ragweed and panic grass are unending sources of food for wildlife.

• Butterflies also prefer weeds and wildflowers. They are attracted to the color purple first, but find yellow, pink and white flowers appealing as well.

• Hummingbirds are drawn to bright, tubular flowers like fuchsia, honeysuckle and trumpet creepers.

• Animals appreciate supplemental feedings in the winter, and for many bird species, these offerings may be essential to survival. If you decide to feed birds, start in the fall and continue through the early spring when there are more natural food sources available.

• Choose feeders that are easy to fill and clean. Place them so you can see them from your house, but be sure to choose a space that is clear of shrubby undergrowth so birds can see approaching cats. Also, put feeders no more than 5 feet from cover to provide feeder birds protection from hawks.

• Offer only fresh, mold-free food and keep feeding areas clean to prevent the possible spread of disease.

• Squirrels can present problems at feeding stations, especially if you hang feeders within their capable reach. Try using baffles or squirrel spooker poles. If all else fails, know that these energetic and persistent animals can be distracted with creative diversions like the "Squirrel-A-Whirl" or their own special feeders available through bird feeder catalogues.

PROVIDING WATER

• A reliable source of fresh, clean water is essential to all living creatures. If you have the right space, consider adding a small pond or fountain to your garden. However, an old-fashioned bird bath, especially one made of aggregate, is just as effective.

• Site water sources close to protective cover. Plan to scrub and refill birdbaths regularly. And remember that animals need water during the winter. If you live in a cold climate, you can keep water ice-free with an immersion heater, but never use antifreeze, which is highly toxic.

POTENTIAL DANGERS
TO BACKYARD WILDLIFE

• Domestic cats pose a tremendous threat to small birds and mammals. If you live with cats, consider keeping them indoors for their own health as well as that of vulnerable wildlife. Should you decide to let them roam, put bells on their collars and ask your neighbors to do the same with their companion animals.

• Birds often see the reflection of their surroundings in windows and fly directly into the glass. Prevent these potentially fatal crashes by hanging the silhouette of a diving hawk on the outside of the window.

SOME FINAL NOTES

• If you live in the city and have nowhere to garden, you can still help wildlife. Urban birds greatly appreciate supplemental winter feedings, even from a small feeder suspended outside an apartment window. You might also help set up or maintain a sanctuary for wildlife wherever you can plant a small garden. Parks, schools, community centers, retirement or convalescent facilities and green belts are just some possibilities.

• And no matter where you live, be sure to share your enthusiasm for wildlife with your friends and neighbors. You have a much better chance of attracting wild animals if your whole neighborhood grows wild. Gardening for wildlife is not just for the animals — it is for you, too. Enjoy!

ABOUT THE AUTHOR

Constance Perenyi holds a degree in Art, and certification in Bird Biology from Cornell University. She has been trained in horticultural design and has taught children her crafted paper techniques at the Washington State Woodland Park Zoo. Her work has been published in *Living Bird Quarterly, Horticulture Magazine* and *Orion* magazines. Constance maintains her own garden in Seattle, Washington, and teaches children around the world about appreciating nature and the wildlife that surrounds them.

ABOUT THE PUBLISHER

Beyond Words Publishing Inc.'s mission is to produce books and related products of high quality and distinctive character while advancing human understanding, to encourage appreciation of nature and the environment, to contribute to international caring and cooperation and through these to enrich the human experience in an interdependent world.

Resources For Your Library

Books About Plants and Animals

• *Golden Guides* (Golden Press, New York) offer pocket-sized field guides to a variety of North American plants and animals.

• *Peterson First Guides,* by Roger Tory Peterson (Houghton Mifflin Co., Boston) are simplified field guides to the birds and mammals of North America.

• *Eyewitness Books* (Alfred A. Knopf, New York) cover the natural histories of the *Bird, Butterfly and Moth,* and *Tree.* For younger readers, *Eyewitness Juniors* offers *Amazing Spiders,* among several other titles.

• *A Kid's First Book of Birdwatching,* by Scott Weidensaul (Running Press, Philadelphia) comes with an audio tape of songbirds.

Books to Introduce Children to Gardening

• *Let's Grow! 72 Gardening Adventures With Children,* by Linda Tilger (Storey Communications, Pownal, Vermont).

• *A Kid's First Book of Gardening,* by Derek Fell (Running Press, Philadelphia).

• *The National Gardening Association Guide to Kids' Gardening,* by Lynn Ocone and Eve Pranis (John Wiley and Sons, New York).

Two of Many Excellent Books
About Gardening for Wildlife

• *The Audubon Society Guide to Attracting Birds,* by Stephen Kress (Charles Scribner's Sons, New York).

• *How To Make A Wildlife Garden,* by Chris Baines (Elm Tree Books, London).

Books to Inspire Appreciation and Respect of Nature

• *Sharing Nature With Children, Sharing the Joy of Nature,* and *Listening to Nature,* all by Joseph Cornell (Dawn Publications, Nevada City, California).

• *Save the Animals!,* by Ingrid Newkirk (Warner Books, New York).

Organizations

To certify your yard as a Backyard Wildlife Habitat, contact:
National Wildlife Federation
1412 16th Street NW
Washington, DC 20036.

For information about joining your local Audubon Society chapter, contact:
National Audubon Society
950 Third Ave.
New York, NY 10022

To learn more about counting birds at winter feeders, contact:
Project Feeder Watch
Cornell Laboratory of Ornithology
159 Sapsucker Woods Road
Ithaca, NY 14850